because it's so weird to think that we
pass so many faces in so many crowds
and they're looking for the same exact
sign that we are.

the beginning to an end

© by the author of this book. The book author retains sole copyright to his or her contributions to this book.

The Blurb-provided layout designs and graphic elements are copyright Blurb Inc. This book was created using the Blurb creative publishing service. The book author retains sole copyright to his or her contributions to this book.

the beginning to an end.

shan

You pushed me off of that cliff.

These are my thoughts on the way down.

Thank you.

9/19/16

9/19/16

I hate you.

I love you.

I actually miss being
heartbroken over you;
being trapped in
eternal misery and
clutching the bars
is much more
comfortable than being
lost and watching for
cars that don't
stop coming.

Please stay away from me.
The walls I've built
around my mind aren't
strong and I'm afraid
you might be able
to break them down
again.
That is something
I cannot handle.
So, please,
act as if
I am a deadly virus
and stay away
even though you're
the thing killing me.

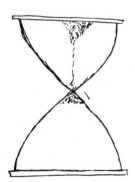

YOUR SKIN IS MY CANVAS
AND MY LIPSTICK IS THE
PAINT SO MY LIPS ARE
THE BRUSH.

S E L F I S H:

   Your 'love' for me was selfish. You only cared about the person in the mirror, you only cared about playing victim while hiding the knife behind your back. You were selfish because you kept the happy pills and the sunlight to yourself, leaving me with a pitch black room and a bittersweet substitute for love. You only cared about your future and what you would do but while I was listening to your unrealistic expectations of a life, I was trying to figure out my own. But I bet you didn't know that because the twenty three hours, fifty six minutes, and four seconds of the day had to be focused on you. I told you about the day not being exactly twenty four hours long but I bet you didn't even remember that. Do you remember anything about me? No. I'm not forgettable. I am not that meaningless. You just view yourself as some sort of god.

From the broken lips of a teenage poet fall the words of a person, who learned just how hard life was way too early.

With bloodshot eyes, looking in the same mirror on different days, the poet says "today" and looks out the window at the gray clouds, hoping that the sun will show up that day. The air is cold and tugs at their skin and their jacket doesn't protect them much- They were never cold when he was there. They didn't need protection. The clouds rolled in when he walked out. Today was another day without the sun and the world seemed to get darker with every 1,440 minutes that passed. Though it never rained. It didn't storm. The weather was frozen. The poet found themselves missing the rain too. However, at 4:30 A.M. the next morning, they woke up and tears started to fall from their eyes as they mourned every ember of feeling they lost. Their eyes were the clouds, their tears were the rain, and the sun came out that day.

I smiled today-

A genuine, honest-

to God smile. It

caused my heart

to beat quickly

and laughter

to crawl up my

throat until it

was bubbling

from the cracked

lips that were

too used to

the words

"Come back."

"I need you."

"Don't leave me."

"Please stop."

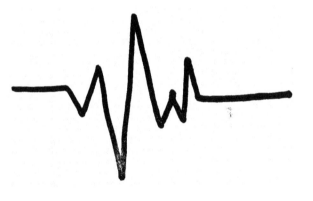

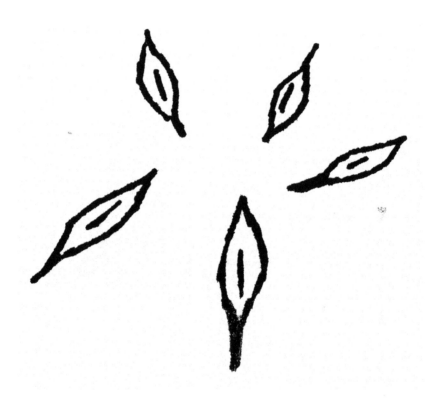

THE LEAVES ARE
CHANGING
AND I'M SO
        ALONE.

I want to be my shadow.

My shadow is taller than me,

My shadow is skinnier than me. My shadow

Is better than me.

My shadow doesn't have

A brain. My shadow

Can't overthink, my shadow doesn't have a heart.

My shadow can't feel it break.

My shadow can't feel.

My shadow can't be scared,

Or sad, or in love;

I want to be my shadow.

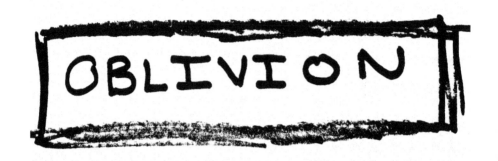

Somehow, I feel so
FUCKING
Oblivious when I'm
Watching you ruin
Everything.

It's like I
Refuse to
ACKNOWLEDGE
Your addiction
To
Destruction.

Every story has

A protagonist,

  The hero.

An antagonist,

  The villain,

And a lover.

My lover became the villain,

And the hero was

Nowhere to be seen.

So please save me because I don't think I'm ready to

take on the role as my own hero.

AS WE RAN FROM THE COPS . . .

Hand in hand, our shoes fighting a war with the pavement, our
breathing working like old machinery.

Our laughs created midnight melodies in parks where
innocence was
sacred, our sins following; clinging to our shadows.

Our eyes swinging to each other and up ahead, our irises
flooded with adrenaline. With happiness. Something we'd been
searching for in green
glass bottles and orange ones with yellow warning labels.

So, to find ecstasy and a reason to live, I'll be chased by
flashing lights,
red and blue, every night as long as you're with me.

1:31 P.M.

bloodstained hands,
tear-dried cheeks.
an angel's grace,
broken from a fall.
words spoken of love,
laced with lies,
and bargaining.

And each time the door opens and a breathing body walks
out,
(though some do not leave breathing) the world gets a bit
darker and
the sun starts to lose its shine. When you lose a lover, a
friend- time.
The day you grow up and you realize life is fragile and so
are you but at
the same time, you're invincible. Nothing can hurt you.
Nothing can
destroy you- only yourself. But when/if you get to that
point, it all
crumbles and you don't really know if you can find
yourself among
the dust and the rubble.

ANIMOSITY:
STRONG HOSTILITY

Words spit like bullets, injecting animosity into the air like a toxin. The feeling cuts through the silence of a Sunday morning. Animosity is defined as strong hostility and it is suffocating. From behind the bars of a prison cell, from high school students vying for attention, from a human being trying to force their way into a place in the world (not necessarily theirs,) the world can push towards peace and towards calmness but animosity will always be hiding in the world's shadow and making sure it is always included in everything the world might do.

CONDESCENDING

Why is everything you do so condescending? Your makeshift crown and imaginary throne makes you believe that you are truly a king, that you are
P E R F E C T and untouchable. Perhaps you are. Maybe you are someone who cannot be touched. But it is not because of your made up superiority; it is because you punish those who don't kneel before you- you treat them as if they are heathens and as if they just spit in your face. Your condescending speeches are constantly repeating in my head-

Like a voicemail that can't be fucking deleted, like a CD or a record that only skips on a certain part and never moves forward and refuses to go back.

I hear these words every damn day but I will **not** bow down to you.

because i swear
there's nothing scarier
than risking spending
life in permanent
heartache.

"Would you like some sugar with your coffee?"
"Yes, please! It'll make it taste better."

"Cream?"
"No thank you, coffee is horrible if it's not dark."

"The weather is so horrible today- Hopefully the sun comes out later on."
"It'll probably storm."

"Do you believe in true love?"
"No. Of course not."

The ****** looked over at the ****** and sighed.

"It will get better."

"I know. I don't want it to."

Happiness
Is a
Mystery
Because to some,
It is love.

To others,
It is a pill
Bottle side
Effect. And to
Others, it is a

Fabrication
Of the
media's
storytelling.

You were Iago and I was your ignorant Emilia.

I did whatever you asked in search for the slightest amount
of love, the smallest gestures of romance.

But I have learned that you are true evil; destroying others,
destroying
people and their lives is just a game to you.

I do not wish to play along. I do not wish to go with or
against you.

And our story is not over yet, for I will tell the world or your
sins and will not look to you for love any longer.

But there's no telling
How it'll end.
My blood on your hands,
Or your blood
Spilling due to
Mine.

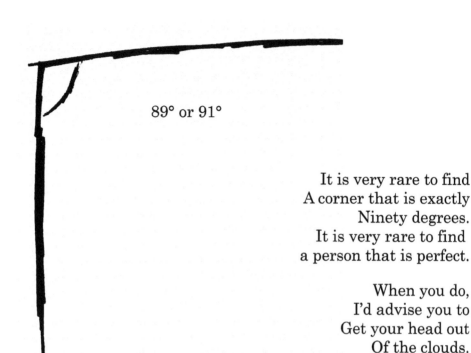

89° or 91°

It is very rare to find
A corner that is exactly
Ninety degrees.
It is very rare to find
a person that is perfect.

When you do,
I'd advise you to
Get your head out
Of the clouds.

Ninety degrees does exist.

Perfect people don't.

FALL

as the leaves changed
colors and the
weather began to
chill, i found
myself
deserted
in a field of
dead trees and

nothing.

WATCHING YOU WITH SOMEONE ELSE

IS LIKE LIGHTING A CIGARETTE.

IT BURNS AND IT DOESN'T STOP

UNTIL MY LIPS HAVE CAUGHT

ON FIRE FROM HOW MUCH

I'M BEGGING FOR YOU.

"You know, I think my biggest fear is . . . is dying alone. Unloved. Unwanted."

"I mean- People love me and care. I know that. But... I miss the feeling of being amazing to someone. I want their heart to clench when they see me
and I want them to- Fuck, I just want someone to look at me and say
'I can't live without you and- I-"

"I hate me. I'll talk to you later."

Please leave a message after the tone.

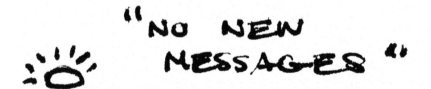

I'm tired of spouting words pumped with love- fucking sonnets- only to get back silence,

literally nothing when I just poured my heart out at your feet. I'm tired of telling you how much I've wanted to have you, to hold and kiss you, fuck I am

IN   LOVE

WITH   YOU

But you're so blind or blissfully fucking ignorant that you can't see that.

So for the love of fuck, can you open your eyes for me and tell me if I'm wasting the time on this clock?

the stars in your eyes
are starting to dim and
i'm so scared to see what
happens when the clouds come
in and your soul is
closed to me forever.
please don't let the
storms break in.

the clouds want to
take you away but
i'm not going to
let them-

i am personally sick of promises
and i am publicly sick of pain.

I'm dead but my heart's still beating.

I have a heart but I can't seem to feel anymore.

My eyes reflect light and my eyes still shine but my spark is gone.

My pulse feels weak and so am I.

You've committed the perfect crime.

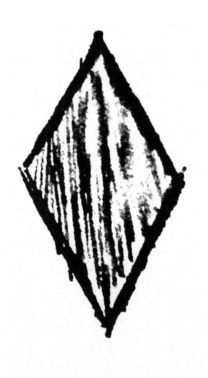

shan

All you guys care about is
Dealing dope
And pouring poison down
Your throat.

All I care about is getting
Cash and finding some way
Out, whether it's by bus or hearse.

The snow has
fallen.

Still alone.

"Revolt!" They yelled. "Rebel."

With voices that created cracks in the seemingly fragile
ground, they raised

hands that could fight off anything and anyone, and they
began a war.

But outside of the battlefield she called her mind,
it was silent.

"SEX! VIOLENCE! REVOLT! ANARCHY! MAYHEM! CHAOS!"

These are the common themes amongst mislead teens;

Teenagers who found the first sign of 'help' that they thought they

needed.

They didn't.

Disguised as 'help', sin took its place.

And now we're all lost in some fucking part of space.

<u>S U R V I V O R</u>

Would you call someone who constantly had a smile on their face a survivor?

Or someone who walked out of the hospital with bandages on their wrists?

What is a survivor to you- Are you a survivor?

Have you pushed yourself through things that people have nightmares about?

Things that people never speak about out loud?

Have you ever lived? You may be alive but are you living?

Truthfully,
I don't care
Nor does it
Matter how
Many times
You say it
To me,

          For I
          Will not
          Believe
          It because
          I am a mirror
          That has been
          Shattered

                    And that
                    Means the
                    Words will
                    Slip through
                    The cracks
                    And I can't
                    Grasp them.

shan

Writing is like

A universe

And every

Genre is a galaxy

And every author

Is a star!

Anyone can be a writer

But not everyone can

Make their words

Make you feel.

BUT THIS IS WHAT
YOU WANTED;
RIGHT?

THIS IS WHAT YOU
DREAMED ABOUT, CRAVED,
FUCKING WENT ON AND
ON ABOUT.

THIS IS WHAT YOU
FUCKING WISHED
FOR SO WHY ARE
YOU LOOKING THE
OTHER FUCKING
W A Y?

If one screw goes loose,
Nothing happens.
If two screws go loose,
Nothing happens.
If three screws go loose,
Maybe something
Will happen.
If four screws go loose,
Hell freezes over
And it all
Falls
D
O
W
N.

TREMORS.

EARTHQUAKES.

PHONE BUZZING.

3 AM BREAKDOWNS WHERE
YOU CAN'T BREATHE AND
YOUR THROAT'S CLOSING
AND YOU'RE
SCREAMING
"WHAT'S GOING ON?!"

NO ONE ANSWERS.

IS THERE EVER AN ANSWER?

PHONE SITS STILL.

GROUND STOPS MOVING.

where are you?

But you painted the
Scarlet fucking letter
On me because
I don't have any
Blood, a soul, a heart, or
Hope to give to you anymore.
You take
And take
And
Take
But you gave me

A reason to disappear.

A reason to give up.

A reason to sit on the edge of a cliff
And fall off.

shan

We are interchangeable.
We are able to be replaced.
Nothing is permanent and
Nothing is for sure.
In the end, there is always someone
Better and all you can do is
Watch as they cut the strings
And, as a worthless puppet,
You fall and they walk away.
It doesn't change.

It does not make a difference.

A coin has two sides, as we all know.
They're completely different but you can tell it's a coin.

People are coins.
People show one sides
But will always have
Another that is seemingly
The opposite of them;
It couldn't possibly be them.

But it is and it's scary
When the coin lands on
That side.

she had raindrops
on her lips

he had a sunshine
in his eyes

she was the type
to ride her
bike through
the streets
of London
while
running
from her
earthquake
of a life

he was the
type
to see her world combust

and sweep
the
ashes under
the carpet.

the beginning to an end

i know that i am **nothing**
without *love*;
i am nothing without
you.

the world is cold and i
am so numb but you walk into my life
and i suddenly
remember what being
alive is like.

"I think this is how I'll
be for the rest of my life;
Pessimistic,
Poetic,
Pathetic."
I could be that teenage poet
who whines about how her
parents don't care and the
boy she loves doesn't want her
and her friends care a little too much.
but i'm tired and i don't
feel like
coming up with the
right words anymore.

_5:02 PM_

I THOUGHT I TOLD MYSELF
I'D NEVER BE THE GIRL
WHO CRIES AND BEGS FOR A BOY TO LOVE HER
BUT
WE ALL BREAK PROMISES AND NOW
I'M BEGGING YOU:

LOVE ME.

BUT YOU WON'T AND THAT'S OKAY;
IT'S FINE.

I WON'T BE OKAY, I WON'T BE ALRIGHT,
BUT WHATEVER
HELPS YOU.

since that seems to be all i'm here for.

right?

i think im dying.
im not sick
but my eyes
feel hollow
and i can't
smile anymore
so i
think im
dying.

BECAUSE A SHOWER
WON'T WASH AWAY
MY SINS

AND A SCENERY
WON'T ERASE
THE WORDS
YOU WROTE

AND A SONG
WON'T COVER
THE SOUND OF
MY HEARTBROKEN SOBS

AND A SWEET
WON'T REPLACE
THE SICK TASTE
ON MY TONGUE

AND A SUN
ON A HOT DAY
WON'T MAKE ME GO OUTSIDE
AND SMELL
THE FUCKING
ROSES

HONESTLY, WHAT WILL?

it's not a case of
unrequited
love.

it's a case of
"i love you and
i won't leave"

in which you **_lied_**
you
don't tell someone
you love
them
if you're just going
to leave
when someone
better looking
comes along.

THESE FOUR WALLS

Repetitive. Constant.
What I wake up to
And sleep staring at.

And when I leave them,
And my walls fall down,
There's no telling if I run scared
Or put on the mask
That says I don't
Belong to these words
And they don't belong to me.

But when the walls
Come back up, so do
The chains around
My neck,
Bestowed by these words.

I'm in love with the noise.

I'm in love with the sound of the waves crashing against the cliff I put myself on.

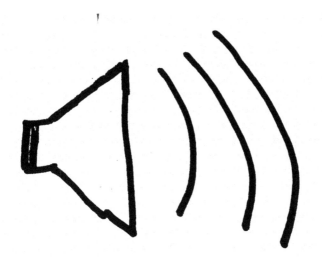

I WISH I COULD BURN THIS BOOK

BECAUSE YOU'D THINK

EVERY WORD IS ABOUT YOU.

but this book is my heart and i do not

wish to die by f i r e.

shan

My problem is that
                I **know** you.

You never took the chance
Nor time
                To tell me I was something.

Unless my feet were planted on the last two inches of a cliff
above a raging ocean, I don't think you thought I was amazing.

At all.

My problem is that I know you.

And I hate the way that I love you because I hate everything
that you are.

WITH EACH PIANO KEY
COMES A TEAR
AND WITH EACH
TEAR
COMES ONE MORE STEP CLOSER

TO WHATEVER I'M FUCKING
RUNNING TOWARDS.

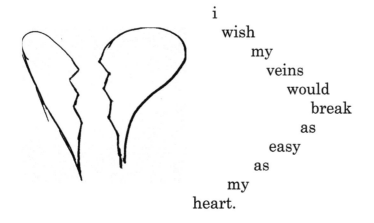

i
  wish
      my
          veins
              would
                  break
                      as
                  easy
              as
          my
heart.

did you notice that
the drawings disappeared?

yeah.

i can't **see** beauty
anymore but
i can still
attempt
to write
it.

there's makeup still left on her
eyes
and she's leaving her disheveled
hair just the way it is.
snow reflects against her eyes
and brightens the expensive depression
her face wears.

it is her favorite time of
year
and now she doesn't
know if she will live
through it.

MY STORY IS THE AFTERMATH

OF A HAPPY ENDING THAT

WENT OFF OF THE RAILS.

I AM THE PRODUCT OF

A PAINTING, *A M A S T E R P I E C E,*

BEING FUCKING BURNED

TO NOTHING BUT ASHES.

there were

poems carved onto her heart,

as well as

her lips.

and he told her

(despite the fact he despised poetry)

to let him read them.

- i used to love sleeping when
it rained.
but i tossed and turned last night
despite the rain
pounding outside
my window but i think it was
the storms inside
my head
because there
aren't any
more sunny
days for
me.

the rain hasn't left
but it's not the
good rain

it's the rain that you drown in

oh god i think i'm drowning

don't pull me out.

shan

You decided that
You did not like
The way
Our names
Fit together
So you tore
Them apart
and
Ripped mine
to shreds.

i don't know who i am.

did i ever?

YOU ARE N O T
THE BOY TO HOLD
A GIRL'S BOOKS

OR TO DISREGARD
SOMEONE'S LOOKS

THE CLICHE BAD BOY TYPE-
THE ONE WITH A GUITAR

AND A LEATHER JACKET.

YOU ARE.

SO WHY DO I WANT YOU SO BAD?

STOP AIMING
your guns
there are
HOLES IN
every part of
MY HEART.

holy crap can i stop being so *s a d* all of the time?

the beginning to an end

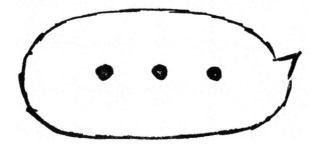

shan

i could say that i'll grow up from this but i grew
up with this. so i guess i'm stuck?

the beginning to an end

loneliness was my gift
until the day
i realized i couldn't
return it.

shan

**THE TREES, THE FLOWERS,
AND LEAVES
ARE DEAD**

AND I'M STILL SO FUCKING ALONE.

i am so not mad
and it
surprises me
that instead
of being out
for blood,
i'd rather see
mine spill.

or yours.

that's okay, too.

I can find words in a dictionary or a book

But I can't find mine and it's killing me, honestly.

Please come back.

Everyone else is making a future for themselves right now and I'm still trying to find the words to open this stupid heart so I can inject this numb, tortured feeling somewhere else.

As strong as you claim I am, I can't do it anymore.

i mention crying over you a lot
but i can't remember
the last time
i cried.

be patient.

the sun went down.

                               do you remember me?

the moon came out.

                                   do you still care?

my cup of coffee is cold.

                          have you noticed i'm gone?

the sun came up.

                                         no.

?

shan

I'm so sad.

        And I can't
        feel it
        anymore.

I wish I could at least feel how sad I was so I wouldn't have meaningless words anymore.

But can you feel without a soul?

I seem to have misplaced mine.

I think I lost it among the words I wrote when imagination broke and reality smiled at me.

I think
I'm scared
to love.
I hesitate
When I
Say I
Love a
Person back.
But I
Love so
Easily.

It's time to wake up.

shan

Alright. Fine.
I'll play the
Sad teenager
Who hates her life
And whines about it all
Damn day.

You be the reason why.

S C R E W

a small piece of metal

meant to hold things together

but would you look at that?

it fucked up because

my mind's falling apart

and my life

is in ruins

and it's all just

spilling out

but i can't believe that you've

managed to do this to me,

you fucking screw.

YOU'RE *EVERYTHING* TO ME.

I WISH YOU WERE *DEAD.*

there is no reason for me to be like this but
i still am this way
and to pretend as if i chose this-

no one would choose this.

if you'd choose this. . .

what the fuck, man?

fuck.

the beginning to an end

Since when did my focus go towards trying to

Forget about you when it should go

Towards trying to find a reason

To live?

Sex.

    SEX!

             One of the human race's biggest
desires.

Not all, but most.

The feeling-   The adrenaline

Of . . .   Running through . . .

Your veins, pumping with the excitement of someone's
hands all over you-

Of your name passing through their lips like prayer.

Calling out God's name because that moment is just so
heavenly ... or it's a moment that would deem you a s i n n
e r for just even imagining it.

You know,
Hearts don't fucking
Work like
Timeshares.

You can't just decide
To love me for
A week and then
Suddenly move on to him.

I never used you.

I gave you
Everything
But it's not enough for you.
Nothing is.
I wasn't, she wasn't.
They aren't.

Go fuck yourself!

it's all white noise.

everything.

i can't focus.

holy shit, i think i hate you-

no. no, i do.

i hope your life crashes down,

like mine did.

melodramatic

if you have ever told your parents you hated them because they couldn't buy you a ridiculously overpriced phone,

or you've broken up with someone for wearing their hair a certain way (yes. it has happened.)

or you've claimed you'll take your life because somebody dared to call you a bad name

or you've fought someone for wearing the same color shirt as you
or you've posted things on social media that worry people on purpose because *you* fucked up and you're not the victim . . .

are you reading this to find out what melodramatic means?

have you done any of these things?

if no, flip the page. if yes, look in the mirror.

that's what melodramatic means.

so please do us all a favor and ***grow the hell up.***

when i look at the ring i

just decided to wear on my

left ring finger,

         i imagine being ***married.***

it's not a goal in my life, i've never fantasized about it.

i couldn't care less.

but maybe being

   happy . . .

IT'S BEEN NEARLY FIVE MONTHS,
THAT BROKEN-LIPPED TEENAGE POET, WHO STARTED
THIS THINKING THEY WOULD NOT FINISH, HAS
NEARLY FILLED UP ALL OF THE PAGES. YEARS AFTER
MEETING THE BIGGEST MISTAKE SHE MADE, SHE
FINALLY REALIZED THAT SHE WAS NOTHING TO THEM.

ABSOLUTELY NOTHING.

BUT THAT'S O K A Y.

MEANING SOMETHING TO HIM ISN'T HER BIGGEST
DESIRE ANYMORE. THE FACT THAT HER VEINS ARE
STILL INTACT ISN'T BECAUSE OF HIM. HER HEART,
THOUGH WEAK, ISN'T BEATING BECAUSE OF HIM.

THE ONLY THING HE'S RESPONSIBLE FOR IS CREATING
A WHOLE NEW WORLD TO PUT ON HER BACK. SHE
MIGHT NOT MAKE IT THROUGH THIS.

SHE COULD GIVE UP AND FALL ANY DAY NOW.

BUT IF SHE FALLS, SHE FALLS KNOWING THAT SHE
DOESN'T NEED NOR W A N T

HIS LOVE, HIS CARE, HIS L O Y A L T Y.
SHE BARELY HAD IT IN THE FIRST PLACE, WHY WOULD
SHE WANT IT NOW?

. . . .

REALLY, SHE JUST WANTS TO CONNECT

THE STARS IN HER SKY

TO MAKE CONSTELLATIONS . . .

TO MAKE HER LEGACY.

i can feel it again.
the rush-
the beating drums in my veins,
the marathon
my heart is running.

oh god, i can *feel* again

i can feel the pain
and the shock
but i can also feel

hope?

The rain
came back but
I'm trying
to turn it into
the background noise
I used to love.

Maybe rain *is* an angel's tears;

an angel who feels that they have
failed the one they have
watched over.

but- whatever the rain may be-
it does not always stay.

the sun will rise.

okay but
WHAT
was *my* sin?

you've never told
me what i've done
so wrong
but you've had
no problem
standing
on your <u>ego</u> to
look down on everyone

and point at
me

and claim

that <u>i've</u> blood on *my* hands.

but all you've done is attempt to wash your own.

DISCLAIMER:

MY TEARS, WORDS,
HEART,

THEY ARE <u>NOT</u> YOURS.

You have Christmas
lights in your eyes.

And a Valentine
in your words.

And a scary story
In your mind

(Your creativity, darling.)

- You're my every holiday

And I like to think you
feel like home.

i don't need you to love me and i feel as though that

is my biggest achievement.

I forgot about you for a day.

One day can become two and as the sun

Keeps rising and the sun

Keeps setting,

One day,

I won't think about you anymore.

i found myself
in the
lipstick stain
on my coffee cup.

after not knowing who i was,

who i really was,

for years

and hating my

unidentifiable self.

i hope i start to love myself.

those two lines of red lipstick

tell me that i just might.

My heart is heavy as I finish this book.

As I finish opening my heart

And letting the words

Fall out

Onto the lines.

It's the beginning of an end but not the final end.

the beginning to an end

If my life is a storybook,

Here it is.

Condensed into

Under 200 pages.

You are the villain.

The criminal.

The words you carved into

my heart won't leave but

you bet your fucking ass I'll

make sure the whole world knows.

Because depression is a new trend and bruised knees is a new fashion and knowing complex, useless formulas over basic, necessary functions is intelligence.

Being sad everyday is not cool.

Acting like sex is a solution is not fashionable.

Having straight A's in a flawed system rather than knowing how to survive on your own is not impressive.

Wanting to live- Having the will to...

That is.

My angst is not important.

I am seventeen.

I am brokenhearted and a bit overdramatic.

I'm a walking Holden Caulfield.

But my angst is not important. It wasn't written for pity.

If you relate to it, good for you.

If you don't, you're lucky.

But this is my heart. This is a corner of my mind, dusted off and ready to be read.

This is me.

My angst is not important but my feelings are.

shan

4:30 AM.

goodnight.

this book is about me.
this book is about you.
this book is about everyone and anyone.
there is no "you." for me, yes, but your 'you' might be different than mine.
you might not have one.

this is the beginning of an end. the end of my teenage angst years. the end of my "it'll never get better for me" period. this is the beginning of my end.

thank you for reading.

(it gets better.)

- shan

2/1/17

Lightning Source UK Ltd.
Milton Keynes UK
UKHW020953090619
344088UK00005B/115/P